WOULD YOU

YOU *FAMILY EDITION*

RATHER?

200+ SILLY, FUN, HILARIOUS
QUESTIONS FOR THE WHOLE FAMILY
TO ENJOY TOGETHER

MADE EASY PRESS

Producer & International Distributor
eBookPro Publishing
www.ebook-pro.com

Would You Rather? Family Edition:
200+ Silly, Fun, Hilarious Questions for the Whole Familyto Enjoy Together

Cover and Illustrations: Maria Sokhatski

Contact: agency@ebook-pro.com
ISBN

HOW TO PLAY

"Would You Rather: Family Edition"

Would You Rather is a fun, simple game for the whole family to play together. Whether you're going on a road trip, having a family gathering, or simply sitting down to family game night, *Would You Rather* is a hilarious, creative, fun activity that you can play again and again!

Who Can Play?

Anyone can play this family-friendly edition of the popular game – kids, parents, grandparents, friends. All of the questions are kid-and-family-friendly!

How Many Players Do You Need?

You need at least two players to properly play the game, but there is no such thing as too many players! You can even read the book on your own if you want to, it just won't really feel like a game, more like a personal challenge.

The Questions

This book has ten sections, each featuring twenty Would You Rather questions. Each question will present you with two funny, weird, or thought-provoking choices to consider.

The Rules

Each round, choose one person to be the judge. After the first round, we recommend you go around the circle in a clockwise direction.

The judge looks at the page and asks everyone the Would You Rather question out loud. For example:

Would you rather be able to jump as far as a kangaroo or be able to swim as fast as a whale?

Give everyone a minute to think about their answer, and then go around the table with everyone explaining what they would choose, and why.

This is where you can get creative – try to think of the smartest, funniest, and silliest explanations, because the person whose answer is deemed best by the judge will win the round!

After everyone has given their answer, the judge rules who gave the best answer and that person receives one point.

Use a piece of paper or a whiteboard to keep score every round!

The Winner

You can choose to play just one section or the whole book – either way, once you're done, tally up the points from all the rounds to see who the winner is!

2-Player Game

If you are playing with only two players, take turns being the judge each time. Give each other points between 1 and 3, according to how much you liked the answer. At the end of the game, the player with the most points wins.

Group Variation

Another way to play the game is in two groups. If there are a lot of players, say more than 8, you can divide up into two teams and play against one another. In this version of the game, one of the teams will ask the question and the other team will have to come up with an answer that they all agree on. The first team will then give them a score from 1 to 3, just like in the two-player game. Change turns after each question and count up the points as usual at the end of the game to see which team is the winner.

Would you rather...

Find a worm in your salad

or

Find a spider in your French fries?

Would you rather...

Eat all your meals at home
and never eat out

or

Eat all your meals out
and never eat at home?

Would you rather...

Eat eggs for breakfast every day

or

Never eat eggs again?

Would you rather...

Eat your dinner while hanging upside down

or

Eat your dinner while lying on the floor?

Would you rather...

Eat moldy cheese

or

Eat raw fish?

Would you rather...

Accidentally put soy sauce
on your pancakes

or

Accidentally put maple syrup
on your sushi?

Would you rather...

Give a friend your burger

or

Give a friend all of your fries?

Would you rather...

Learn how to bake a cake

or

Learn how to bake bread?

Would you rather...

Drink soup with a straw
or
Drink water from a bowl?

Would you rather...

Not be able to taste food
or
Not be able to smell food?

Would you rather...

Chew gum that tastes like meat

or

Chew gum that tastes
like vegetables?

Would you rather...

Eat hot ice cream

or

Eat cold apple pie?

Would you rather...

Eat cereal with orange juice
or
Eat rice with chocolate milk?

Would you rather...

Never eat anything sweet again
or
Never eat anything savory again?

Would you rather...

Eat dessert once a month but it's
always your favorite dessert

or

Eat dessert every day but it's
always your least favorite dessert?

Would you rather...

Forget to put sugar in chocolate
chip cookies

or

Forget to put sugar
in chocolate cake?

Would you rather...

Eat something that was in the trash

or

Eat something that was on the floor?

Would you rather...

Eat ten spicy chili peppers

or

Eat ten ice cubes?

Would you rather...

Go to the movies every day
but never get popcorn

or

Go to the movies once a year
but eat as much popcorn as you want?

Would you rather...

Eat twenty tiny meals a day

or

Eat one big meal a day?

Would you rather...

Know how to talk to animals

or

Know how to make
animals obey you?

Would you rather...

Get bitten by a snake

or

Get stung by a scorpion?

Would you rather...

Live in a bird's nest

or

Live in a fox's hole?

Would you rather...

Hug a lion

or

Kiss an alligator?

Would you rather...

Discover dragons are real
or
Discover unicorns are real?

Would you rather...

Have a tail but walk on two legs
or
Not have a tail but walk
on four legs?

Would you rather...

Work as a beekeeper

or

Work as a lion tamer?

Would you rather...

Find yourself in a wrestling
cage with a gorilla

or

Find yourself in a swimming
competition with a dolphin?

Would you rather...

Have fur like a bear

or

Have scaly skin
like a snake?

Would you rather...

Be as small as an ant

or

Be as big as an elephant?

Would you rather...

Be followed around by
a hundred butterflies

or

Be followed around by
a hundred ants?

Would you rather...

Have a tongue as long as a lizard's

or

Have ears as big as a rabbit's?

Would you rather...

Laugh like a hyena
or
Snort like a whale?

Would you rather...

Have a pet dog that eats your clothes
or
Have a pet cat that breaks your toys?

Would you rather...

Scratch yourself like a dog
or
Clean yourself like a cat?

Would you rather...

Have colorful feathers like a peacock
or
Have sharp talons like a falcon?

Would you rather...

Find a mouse in your pocket
or
Find a rat in your backpack?

Would you rather...

Meet a shark in a swimming pool
or
Meet a tiger in the playground?

Would you rather...

Have a hump like a camel
but never be thirsty

or

Have cheeks like a chipmunk
but never be hungry?

Would you rather...

Play a memory game with an elephant

or

Play a staring game with an owl?

Would you rather...

Sit at the front of the class
but know all the answers

or

Sit at the back of the class
but not know any of the answers?

Would you rather...

Repeat the same grade twice
but stay with all your friends

or

Skip a grade but
not have any friends?

Would you rather...

Take a five-minute test every day

or

Take a five-hour test every month?

Would you rather...

Walk to school and get there early

or

Take the bus to school
but get there late?

Would you rather...

Have to go to school
for ten hours every day

or

Have to do chores
for ten hours every day?

Would you rather...

Have to solve a math problem
while standing on your head

or

Have to recite a poem
while underwater?

Would you rather...

Only have science class
for a whole week

or

Only have history class
for a whole week?

Would you rather...

Realize you forgot to study
for a test you have today

or

Realize you forgot
your lunch at home?

Would you rather...

Get an F
but the teacher loves you

or

Get an A
but the teacher hates you?

Would you rather...

Sing in front
of the whole school

or

Dance in front
of the whole school?

Would you rather...

Have shorter recess
and go home earlier

or

Have longer recess
and go home later?

Would you rather...

Get to school and realize
you forgot all your books

or

Get to school and realize
you forgot to wear pants?

Would you rather...

Wear the same clothes
to school every day

or

Wear the same funny hat
to school every day?

Would you rather...

Be sneezing in your school picture

or

Be blinking in your school picture?

Would you rather...

Ride to school every day
with the principal

or

Ride to school every day
with your least favorite teacher?

Would you rather...

Get As in half your classes
and Fs in the other half

or

Get Cs in all your classes?

Would you rather...

Go to school at Hogwarts

or

Go to school in Narnia?

Would you rather...

Wear pajamas to school

or

Wear a suit and tie to school?

Would you rather...

Have a teacher
who is eight feet tall

or

Have a teacher
who is three feet tall?

Would you rather...

Be the most popular kid in school

or

Be the smartest kid in school?

Would you rather...

Sleep in a tent in Antarctica
or
Sleep on a treetop in Brazil?

Would you rather...

Know the names of
all the flowers in the world
or

Know the names of
all the trees in the world?

Would you rather...

Climb Mount Everest
while blindfolded

or

Climb Mount Everest
while handcuffed?

Would you rather...

Live in a place where
it's always hot

or

Live in a place where
it's always cold?

Would you rather...

Visit every country for one hour

or

Visit one country of your choice
for a month?

Would you rather...

Be stranded alone in a forest

or

Be stranded alone
on a desert island?

Would you rather...

Have the window seat
on a plane but no TV

or

Have the aisle seat on a plane
with your own TV?

Would you rather...

Go bungee jumping

or

Go sky diving?

Would you rather...

Have to walk through a muddy swamp
or
Have to walk over an icy lake?

Would you rather...

Make a snowman
without gloves on
or

Build a sandcastle
while wearing gloves?

Would you rather...

Fly to Mars on a spaceship

or

Dive to the bottom of the ocean
in a submarine?

Would you rather...

Visit fifty countries

or

Speak fifty languages?

Would you rather...

Live in a theme park
or
Live in a water park?

Would you rather...

Spend a month in space
or
Spend a month at sea?

Would you rather...

Plant one tree every day

or

Plant one thousand trees
in one week?

Would you rather...

Live on a farm

or

Live in a castle?

Would you rather...

Step in dog poop with bare feet

or

Have a bird poop on your head?

Would you rather...

Live in a zoo

or

Live in an aquarium?

Would you rather...

Eat ice cream in Italy

or

Eat a croissant in France?

Would you rather...

Enter any museum for free

or

Enter any art gallery for free?

Would you rather...

Celebrate Halloween three times a year

or

Celebrate Easter three times a year?

Would you rather...

Have Christmas in the summer

or

Have summer vacation
in the winter?

Would you rather...

Only be able to celebrate
your birthday but not Christmas

or

Only be able to celebrate
Christmas but not your birthday?

Would you rather...

Have to share all your birthday gifts

or

Not get any birthday gifts?

Would you rather...

Go to a birthday party
with smelly socks

or

Go to a birthday party
with messy hair?

Would you rather...

Have three months of summer vacation
but go to school on weekends

or

Go to school four days a week
but have no summer vacation?

Would you rather...

Find a rat in your Christmas tree

or

Find a snake in your
Christmas stocking?

Would you rather...

Meet the Easter Bunny

or

Meet Santa Claus?

Would you rather...

Have the best Christmas tree
in the neighborhood

or

Have the best Christmas lights
in the neighborhood?

Would you rather...

Get one piece of candy
on Valentine's Day

or

Get ten love letters
on Valentine's Day?

Would you rather...

Help Santa wrap all the presents
or
Help Santa deliver all the presents?

Would you rather...

Wrap fifty presents
or
Write fifty cards?

Would you rather...

Eat spinach-flavored ice cream
or
Eat ketchup-flavored ice cream?

Would you rather...

Go on an adventure trip
or
Go on a luxurious holiday?

Would you rather...

Eat a whole birthday cake
or
Eat a whole Thanksgiving turkey?

Would you rather...

Get a pair of socks
for your birthday
or

Get a dictionary
for your birthday?

Would you rather...

Live inside a snow globe

or

Live inside a gingerbread house?

Would you rather...

Go trick-or-treating with Dracula

or

Go trick-or-treating with a ghost?

Would you rather...

Have to chase and catch a live
turkey for Thanksgiving dinner

or

Have to hand-pick five hundred
cranberries to make cranberry sauce?

Would you rather...

Attend a wedding underwater

or

Attend a wedding in space?

Would you rather...

Have every book you
ever wanted for free

or

Have every video game you
ever wanted for free?

Would you rather...

Be the best player
on a bad sports team

or

Be the worst player
on a good sports team?

Would you rather...

Only listen to rock music
for the rest of your life

or

Only listen to classical music
for the rest of your life?

Would you rather...

Only watch cartoons

or

Only watch action movies?

Would you rather...

Be able to jump as far as a kangaroo
or
Be able to swim as fast as a whale?

Would you rather...

Go to the movie theatre
but everyone there stinks
or
Go to watch a baseball game
but everyone there is screaming?

Would you rather...

Play mini golf with
a five-inch golf club

or

Play bowling with
a rubber bowling ball?

Would you rather...

Never play a video again

or

Never use social media again?

Would you rather...

Be able to write super fast

or

Be able to read super fast?

Would you rather...

Have the biggest collection
of stamps in the world

or

Have the biggest collection
of seashells in the world?

Would you rather...

Only watch TV shows
or
Only watch movies?

Would you rather...

Have to practice piano
for five hours a day
or
Have to read
for five hours a day?

Would you rather...

Be embarrassed often
but have a lot of funny stories to tell

or

Never embarrass yourself
but have no funny stories to tell?

Would you rather...

Compete in the Summer Olympics

or

Compete in the Winter Olympics?

Would you rather...

Never watch a movie again

or

Never play a video game again?

Would you rather...

Only be able to text people
and never call them

or

Only be able to call people
and never text them?

Would you rather...

Be the best at one single sport
or
Be slightly better than
average at every sport?

Would you rather...

Read a book you love again
or
Read a brand-new book?

Would you rather...

Have a pilot's license

or

Have a skipper's license?

Would you rather...

Get stuck upside down
on a rollercoaster for one minute

or

Spend an entire rollercoaster ride
unsure whether your seat is safe?

Would you rather...

Lick a trash can

or

Lick the floor?

Would you rather...

Never brush your teeth

or

Never take a shower?

Would you rather...

Chew someone else's old gum

or

Use someone else's toothbrush?

Would you rather...

Have stinky feet

or

Have smelly armpits?

Would you rather...

Fart all the time but
it smells like roses

or

Burp all the time but
it tastes like chocolate?

Would you rather...

Kiss a frog on the mouth

or

Hug a skunk?

Would you rather...

Rub mayonnaise
all over yourself

or

Rub spaghetti sauce
all over yourself?

Would you rather...

Sleep in a bed with
a hundred cockroaches

or

Have a hundred slugs
in your shower?

Would you rather...

Be the ugliest person
in the world

or

Be the worst-smelling
person in the world?

Would you rather...

Be able to see germs

or

Be able to hear lice?

Would you rather...

Take a shower in orange juice
or
Wash your hands in honey?

Would you rather...

Have to always pee outside
or
Have to always poop
in public restrooms?

Would you rather...

Drink spoiled milk
or
Eat spoiled cheese?

Would you rather...

Get to school and realize you are
naked and everyone else is dressed
or
Get to school and realize you are
dressed and everyone else is naked?

Would you rather...

Wear your underwear outside
your clothes for a day

or

Wear the same underwear
for a week?

Would you rather...

Sleep in a dog kennel

or

Eat a bowl of dog food?

Would you rather...

Find a fingernail
in your food

or

Find a clump of hair
in your food?

Would you rather...

Always have boogers hanging
out your nose

or

Always have a big pimple
in the middle of your forehead?

Would you rather...

Have a bucket of slime
poured on your head

or

Have a bucket of mud
poured on your head?

Would you rather...

Put your hand in your pocket
and discover it's filled with Jell-O

or

Put your foot in your shoe and
discover it's filled with chocolate sauce?

Would you rather...

Be the king or queen of a country
or
Be the mayor of a city?

Would you rather...

Earn a high salary but have
to work twelve hours a day
or
Earn a low salary but only have
to work six hours a day?

Would you rather...

Be a very wealthy thief

or

Be a very poor doctor?

Would you rather...

Write a famous book

or

Direct a famous movie?

Would you rather...

Be a professional athlete

or

Be a professional actor or actress?

Would you rather...

Have a job where you have
to stand on your feet all day

or

Have a job where you have to sit
in front of a screen all day?

Would you rather...

Be an FBI special agent but have
to tell everyone you're an accountant

or

Be an accountant but make everyone
think you're an FBI special agent?

Would you rather...

Be the only person
who lives forever

or

Be the only person
who doesn't live forever?

Would you rather...

Work as a soccer coach

or

Work as a soccer referee?

Would you rather...

Be an astronaut but have to live
in space for six months every year

or

Be a wildlife photographer but have to
live in a tent for six months every year?

Would you rather...

Be a cat trapped in a human body

or

Be a human trapped in a cat body?

Would you rather...

Be able to drive any vehicle
you come across

or

Be able to play any instrument
you come across?

Would you rather...

Spend the rest of your
life in prison

or

Spend the rest of your
life as a slave?

Would you rather...

Be the first person
to explore a new planet

or

Invent the cure
for a deadly disease?

Would you rather...

Be a personal chef

or

Be the head chef
at a restaurant?

Would you rather...

Have to drive for two hours
to work every day

or

Have to walk for one hour
to work every day?

Would you rather...

Host a successful podcast

or

Host a successful
YouTube channel?

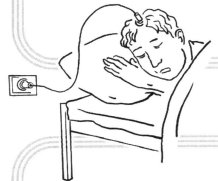

Would you rather...

Have to plug your brain into
a wall socket every night to charge

or

Have to connect your brain
to an alarm clock to wake up?

Would you rather...

Have your dream job
but get no vacation days

or

Have a boring job but get
20 vacation days a year?

Would you rather...

Be the main character in a movie
that no one watches

or

Be an extra with no lines
in a very successful movie?

Would you rather...

Sound like a troll
or
Look like one?

Would you rather...

Always have dirty feet
or
Always have dirty hands?

Would you rather...

Be able to read minds

or

Know how to become
invisible?

Would you rather...

Walk on your hands

or

Eat with your feet?

Would you rather...

Sleep for eighteen hours a day
or
Sleep for eighteen hours a week?

Would you rather...

Be the tallest person in the world
or
Be the shortest person in the world?

Would you rather...

Have three eyes
or
Have two noses?

Would you rather...

Have no eyebrows
or
Have no eyelashes?

Would you rather...

Have pink hair
or
Have blue skin?

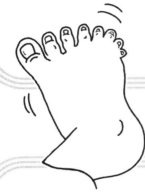

Would you rather...

Have extra fingers
or
Have extra toes?

YOUR BODY

Would you rather...

Breathe from your belly button
or
Sweat from your ears?

Would you rather...

Be able to see through walls
or
Be able to hear from miles away?

Would you rather...

Pee chocolate milk

or

Poop ice cream?

Would you rather...

Fall down every single flight
of stairs

or

Trip over every curb?

Would you rather...

Have long hair that reaches
the floor but is always tangled

or

Be bald?

Would you rather...

Your nose got longer
every time you lied

or

Your ears got bigger
every time you laughed?

Would you rather...

Giggle when you're mad
or
Have smoke come out your
ears when you're happy?

Would you rather...

All your teeth fall out
or
All your hair falls out?

Would you rather...

Have transparent skin
so you can see all your organs

or

Have prickly skin
that hurts to touch?

Would you rather...

Be able to breathe underwater

or

Be able to fly?

Would you rather...

Have a magic wand
that grants wishes

or

Have a magic cloak that
makes you invisible?

Would you rather...

Have a pet phoenix that can
heal you when you get hurt

or

Have a pet dragon that scares
your enemies away?

Would you rather...

Live in a world with elves and fairies
or
Live in a world with robots and aliens?

Would you rather...

Have a talking plant friend
who gives good advice
or
Have a talking animal friend
with a great sense of humor?

Would you rather...

Live in a castle in the sky
or
Live in a cozy Hobbit hole
under the ground?

Would you rather...

Have a magic mirror that
answers every question you ask it
or
Have a crystal ball that
shows you the future?

Would you rather...

Be able to live inside the world
of your favorite fantasy book

or

Be able to live inside the world
of your favorite fantasy movie?

Would you rather...

Have a magic mop that cleans
your entire house

or

Have an enchanted spoon
that cooks all your meals?

Would you rather...

Have a personal wizard assistant

or

Have a genie who can
grant you three wishes?

Would you rather...

Have a never-ending supply
of ice cream

or

Have a never-ending supply
of chocolate?

Would you rather...

Find a secret cave filled
with buried treasure

or

Build your own working
time machine?

Would you rather...

Have a magic backpack that
can hold everything you need

or

Have a magic tent that
is as big as a house inside?

Would you rather...

Be able to transform into any animal

or

Be able to talk to any animal?

Would you rather...

Have a pet dragon

or

Have a pet unicorn?

Would you rather...

Travel to school or work
on a flying carpet

or

Fly to another country
in a flying car?

Would you rather...

Have a garden that grows
chocolate and candy

or

Have a garden that grows
toys and games?

Would you rather...

Be able to make plants
grow faster

or

Be able to control water
with your mind?

Would you rather...

Have a magic door that leads
to different fantasy lands

or

Have a magic wardrobe that leads
to different countries in the world?

Would you rather...

Have dinner with a character
from a horror movie

or

Have dinner with a character
from an animated movie?

Would you rather...

Wear shoes that make you walk
or run twice as fast

or

Wear a hat that tells you what people
around you are thinking?

Would you rather...

Have bedroom walls
that change color every day

or

Have an enchanted ceiling
that shows you the weather outside?

Would you rather...

Have a blanket that keeps you
at the perfect temperature

or

Have a pillow that makes
all of your dreams happy?

Would you rather...

Live in Hansel and Gretel's candy house

or

Live in Cinderella's castle?

Would you rather...

Be able to bring your stories to life

or

Be able to bring your drawings to life?

Printed in Great Britain
by Amazon

35095372R00059